Cover – A group of young Maori perform a haka, a challenge performed traditionally by warriors preparing for battle. (Gaylene Earl, Focus New Zealand)

Front and back endpapers – A replica traditional palisaded Maori village that shows the early form of whare (houses) on the right with an elevated pataka (storehouse) from a later period in the centre. (Peter Bush)

Title page – Contemporary Maori bone carving designs. (In Stock New Zealand)

ISBN 1-86958-139-3

© 1995 Hodder Moa Beckett Publishers Limited

Published in 1995 by Hodder Moa Beckett Publishers Limited
[a member of the Hodder Headline Group]
28 Poland Road, Glenfield, Auckland, New Zealand

Printed through Bookbuilders, Hong Kong

New Zealand Maori

Nobody is totally sure where the Maori came from and when they arrived. Current archaeological evidence suggests that most of the people of the Pacific are related (excluding the indigenous people of Australia and Papua New Guinea), and originated from Southeast Asia perhaps 20,000 years ago. The ancestors of the Maori hopped from island to island in a gradual pilgrimage westward, finally discovering this country in the southern corner of the Pacific about a thousand years ago. These pioneers named the islands "Aotearoa" or "Land of the Long White Cloud", reflecting their first impressions of the new land.

According to tradition, Maori came from a homeland called Hawaiiki, and journeyed to New Zealand in the large double-hulled sailing vessels that were typical of Polynesian ocean-going craft. There are traditionally seven named canoes from whose occupants the various tribes trace their descendants.

In later years the Maori designed the waka taua (war canoes). It was this type of canoe that greeted the Dutchman Abel Tasman. Tasman was the first European to visit these shores in 1642. The explorer James Cook was also met by Maori in waka taua in 1769 when he arrived to chart the New Zealand waters and extensively document his interactions with the Maori.

The Maori that Cook and Tasman encountered were a highly organised tribal people with a social structure based on the whanau (family), hapu (subtribe), and iwi (tribe). The iwi were patriarchal for the most part and lead by rangatira (chiefs) who commanded loyalty by their ability to lead and provide for the people.

The customs and crafts of the Maori had evolved over thousands of years and were at a highly advanced stage when European contact was made. The crafts of the Maori are a source of great pride. Oral tradition has it that carving was introduced to the Maori by Rua, who took some carved poupou (posts) when recovering his captured son from Tangaroa (god of the oceans).

Maori whakairo (carving) styles with Pacific origins have evolved over a thousand years. The isolation of this country, and the abundance of timber like totara and kauri, have resulted in a perfection unmatched in all of Polynesia. Carvings are also created from bone, pounamu (greenstone or nephrite jade) and stone, and like wooden carvings these are often very ornate. Maori spirituality is closely connected with these art forms, and ancestral carvings are considered tapu (sacred).

Raranga (weaving), like carving, is an industry that has roots in the Pacific. The natural resources of Aotearoa have resulted in creations made from harakeke (flax plant). There are more than 30 varieties of harakeke in New Zealand, and the Maori used this material to create a diverse range of items, including taura (rope), kupenga (fishing nets), potae (hats), kete (baskets), whariki (mats) and kahu (cloaks). Kahu were also made from dog skin and a variety of bird feathers.

The word "tattoo" was introduced to the English language by the English sailors of Cook's time, who were tattooed in the Tahitian islands. For the Maori people the practice of wearing moko (bodily and facial tattoos) was said to have been begun by Mataura, whose father-in-law tattooed him when he went into the underworld to look for his wife. The custom is common throughout the Pacific, but the facial tattoo of the Maori is unique.

The blue-green pigment of traditional moko was created by mixing berries and a powder of the pounded charcoal remains of special grubs. The face of the recipient was carved with small chisels, then a second incision was made to colour the grooves with pigment. The ceremony was very tapu because of the spilling of blood. Technology has had an influence nowadays, as the moko are painted temporarily or created with modern tattooing drills.

The performance of waiata (song) has also adopted some contemporary features. These include modern tunes and musical instruments like the guitar. Since the 1920s Maori people have formed concert parties to entertain. Such mana (prestige) is derived from expert kapa haka groups that national competitions are held regularly to decide the performers with the most finesse in bringing the poi (spheres whirled on the ends of strings) to life, the most melodious singing and the fiercest, most awe-inspiring haka.

Although some Maori customs have been lost over time, many remain. Conventions such as wairua Maori (spirituality), whanaungatanga (family belonging), te reo (the language), manaakitanga (hospitality), and the role of the marae are still very important to many Maori, who take pride in and work to preserve the ways of the old people.

A waka taua (war canoe) displayed at Waitangi. These sleek vessels are a source of great pride for the iwi (tribe) which owns them. (Peter Bush)

A man with moko (facial tattoo) that denotes tribal affiliation exchanges a hongi (pressing of noses and salute to the breath of life) with this kuia (female Maori elder).

(Scott Lee, Fotopacific)

Two Maori girls dressed in full traditional costume display the style of moko typically worn by women and the modern taniko headband. (Ted Scott, Focus New Zealand)

F or this man, enduring the pain of the electric drill is less challenging than the hammer-and-chisel tattooing of the old days. (Louis Edward, Fotopacific)

A performer painted with full-face moko for a ceremonial occasion.

(Fotopacific)

This woman entertains with a waiata-a-ringa or action song.

(DAC)

A group of Maori traditionally dressed for a formal occasion join in a waiata (song or chant).

(Gaylene Earl, Focus New Zealand)

These women entertain with the spectacular and dexterous art of the poi dance.

(Brian Moorhead, Focus New Zealand)

Keeping rhythm with a waiata, the rakau (wooden rods) are tossed and spun expertly by this concert party. (Brian Moorhead, Focus New Zealand)

T he awesome power
and passion of a haka.

(Gaylene Earl, Focus New Zealand)

The men of this roopu (group) issue a challenge of defiance in this haka.

(Fotopacific)

Stunning examples of beautiful whare whakairo (carved houses) that are symbols of great mana (prestige) and pride for the iwi. (Peter Bush)

A close view of these flowing carvings shows the carver's skill on a pataka (storehouse), in which food and sometimes valuable ornaments were kept.

(Peter Bush)

The contemporary figure of a tekoteko depicting a tipuna (ancestral leader) of high tribal repute stands astride the more traditional tekoteko of this whare whakairo.

(DAC)

The tekoteko, tahuhu (ridgepole) and heke (rafters) of a whare (house). The whare is said to embody a revered ancestor, the tahuhu is the backbone and the heke are the ribs.

(DAC)

Ohinemutu Marae in Rotorua is a marae
with beautiful whakairo (carvings).

(B. Enting)

The majestic interior of an elaborately carved
and panelled whare whakairo.

(Andris Apse)

These poutokomanawa (centre posts) represent the most significant tipuna of the iwi (tribe). Physically and spiritually they support the local iwi. (Jays, Fotopacific)

The walls of this wharenui (great house) are lined by poupou (pillars) that serve as the iwi records of tipuna and incidents of the past. The poupou are bisected by tukutuku panels of traditional design.

(Julia Thorne, Fotopacific)

This picture shows the relationship and intricate decoration of the tukutuku panels, poutokomanawa and the kowhaiwhai patterns on the tahuhu and heke.

(Brian Moorhead, Focus New Zealand)

The upoko (head) is considered the most tapu (sacred) part of the body by the Maori. For this reason the upoko of many poupou are disproportionately large.

(Brian Moorhead, Focus New Zealand)

The entrance to the marae-atea (courtyard) with the whare whakairo in the background. Visitors to the marae would wait at the entrance to be called onto the marae-atea.

(David Hallet, Fotopacific)

A large haka party challenge manuhiri (visitors) from the marae-atea which is also known as the domain of Tu-matauenga, the god of war. Nowadays the only battles that are common are verbal.

(Rob Tucker, Fotopacific)

The hangi is the indigenous cooking method of the Maori people. Here cooked food that has been steamed in the earth oven for several hours is being lifted. (Tamaki Tours)

The vegetables in the top basket and meat in the
lower basket are cooked to perfection.

(Tamaki Tours)

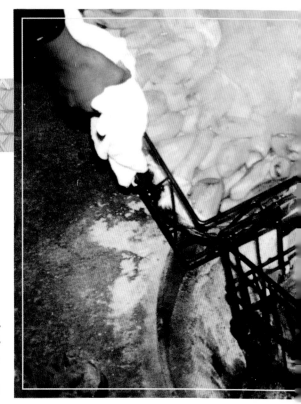

The kumara (sweet potato) is the only item of this succulent meal that is native to the Maori. This picture includes the introduced potato, chicken, pork and mutton of the Pakeha (European).

(Tamaki Tours)

Two carvers work on poupou at the Whakarewarewa Arts and Craft Institute in Rotorua. Women are considered to be noa (free from tapu), therefore the tapu art of whakairo is the responsibility of men. (Peter Bush)

Just as his forebears did in the past, this carver takes great pride in his craft as he concentrates intensely.

(DAC)

One of the rangatahi (younger generation)
learns an art that is centuries old.

(Brian Moorhead, Focus New Zealand)

Flax strips are threaded and woven through the wooden slats of a tukutuku panel to create a symbolic pattern. Raranga (weaving) is usually done by women, using skills learned over a lifetime.

(DAC)

A kahu huruhuru (feather cloak) is woven
by the expert hands of a kuia.

(DAC)

This woman sits in front of the flax bush that has been used to create the potae (hat) and kete (baskets).

(Gaylene Earl, Focus New Zealand)

The piupiu (flax skirts) hanging in the background are made from flax that has been scraped, dried, curled and dyed.

(New Zealand Maori Arts & Crafts Institute)

Three stages of creating a superb bone carving.

(New Zealand Maori Arts & Crafts Institute)

Precious pounamu (nephrite jade) ornaments, which are worn around the neck, surround a mere (traditional hand weapon). Made from jade found in its natural state as river boulders, these pieces have been created by a master carver.

(New Zealand Maori Arts & Crafts Institute)

The beaming grins of these two young Maori boys contrast
with the pukana (wild stare) of the poupou behind.   (Brian Moorhead, Focus New Zealand)

These boys are happy to interrupt their boogie boarding to share their infectious smiles.

(Brian Moorhead, Focus New Zealand)